The Parts of the Pure Stone

Level 6 – Orange

Helpful Hints for Reading at Home

The graphemes (written letters) and phonemes (units of sound) used throughout this series are aligned with Letters and Sounds. This offers a consistent approach to learning whether reading at home or in the classroom.

HERE IS A LIST OF GRAPHEMES FOR THIS PHASE OF LEARNING. AN EXAMPLE OF THE PRONUNCIATION CAN BE FOUND IN BRACKETS.

Phase 5			
ay (day)	ou (out)	ie (tie)	ea (eat)
oy (boy)	ir (girl)	ue (blue)	aw (saw)
wh (when)	ph (photo)	ew (new)	oe (toe)
au (Paul)	a_e (make)	e_e (these)	i_e (like)
o_e (home)	u_e (rule)		

HERE ARE SOME WORDS WHICH YOUR CHILD MAY FIND TRICKY.

Phase 5 Tricky Words			
oh	their	people	Mr
Mrs	looked	called	asked
could			

GPC focus: /o_e/u_e/

TOP TIPS FOR HELPING YOUR CHILD TO READ:

- Allow children time to break down unfamiliar words into units of sound and then encourage children to string these sounds together to create the word.

- Encourage your child to point out any focus phonics when they are used.

- Read through the book more than once to grow confidence.

- Ask simple questions about the text to assess understanding.

- Encourage children to use illustrations as prompts.

This book focuses on the phonemes /o_e/ and /u_e/ and is an orange level 6 book band.

The Parts of the Pure Stone

Written by
Emilie Dufresne

Illustrated by
Rachel Sawyer

There was unrest in the Blue Lands. The tribes had been fighting for land, goods and stone. From the high Mountain Townships, to Fortune Forest...

... the Stone Caves in the Bone Cliffs to the Green Mire – the Blue Lands had the same problems as they had years and years ago.

On a day filled with mist and chill, some of the clans had got into a dispute.
"Get back on your land, Borg!" said Elwin.

"If you had not taken stone from my land, I would not be here!" said Borg.
A whoosh of wings ended the fight.

The gang stood shocked. Dragons were from tales. After the Fight of the Five Lands, there had been no sight of them...

The creature spoke.
"I am Ember. I have come from Reptile's Rook to tell you this. You will take a quest across the Blue Lands."

"You alone must bring together the two parts of the Pure Stone. It was split by the Dark Shades of Gloom. We need it now to fight the Shades again."

"The parts can be found here. Be swift, there is not much time." And with that, Ember rose into the air with one flap and drifted out of sight.

"Are we all in?" asked Pan. They all agreed. "To the Fortune Forests, then!" she yelled as they marched. Elwin marched near Pan.

"The Fortune Forests are my lands. I think a part might be hidden in the True Tree. It is with the Bark Men."

"It is the most powerful tree in all of the forest," said Elwin on seeing it. He ran his hand along its wide trunk.

"When will the Bark Men be here?" asked Zorvak.

"The Bark Men felt our feet and tuned in to our mutterings from just one footstep in the Fortune Forest."

Branches began to crack. A booming sound rang.

"The True Tree told us of this day. You are here for the part of the Pure Stone are you not?"

The Bark Men leaned down to the gang, inspecting them.
"Elwin, you have come with… an orc? Can we trust you and…"

"... this gang... of... of fools to keep the stone safe and secure?"

"You think we are fools? How come that dragon chose us, then?" chirped Pan.

The True Tree began to shine. A bright white light came from a gap, high in the trunk. The Bark Men leaned to the tree.

Without speaking, one of the Bark Men reached into the beam of light, into the True Tree with his hands and took something out.

It was passed to the gang. They put it in their sack. Zorvak slung it across her back. "To the Stone Caves we go," she said.

"The Stone Caves are in the Bone Cliffs near the sea. I bet the second part of the Pure Stone is hidden in the copper stocks, deep in the caves," said Borg.

"The oldest stock is right at the bottom, down here," said Borg, leading them along lines and lines of copper rocks. "Where could it be?"

A white beam of light lit up the cave. The gang rushed to it. There on a shelf, thick with dust, the light from the second part of the Pure Stone streamed onto them.

"Quick, we need to melt them and fuse them together!" said Elwin. They ran to the fires.

The melted stone had set. They broke it open and there stood the silver cube. There was a whoosh and the gang rushed outside with the cube.

"The Pure Stone, you did it. You made a fine team in the end it seems," said Ember.

"The Dark Shades of Gloom are getting stronger as we speak and this cube, no matter how plain and small it may look, may be their downfall."

"Come now, onto my back. We are off to the Mountain Townships!" said Ember, leaning a wing down.

"We are?" asked Borg.

"Odd Bod waits for us there."

The Parts of the Pure Stone

1. What is the dragon's name?

2. Who split the Pure Stone?

3. Who does the gang meet in the Fortune Forests?

   a) The Bark Men

   b) The Branch Boys

   c) The Leaf Ladies

4. How do they put the two parts of the Pure Stone together?

5. What do you think will happen next? Who is Odd Bod?

©2021 **BookLife Publishing Ltd.**
King's Lynn, Norfolk PE30 4LS

ISBN 978-1-83927-417-6

All rights reserved. Printed in Malaysia.
A catalogue record for this book is available from the British Library.

The Parts of Pure Stone
Written by Emilie Dufresne
Illustrated by Rachel Sawyer

An Introduction to BookLife Readers...

Our Readers have been specifically created in line with the London Institute of Education's approach to book banding and are phonetically decodable and ordered to support each phase of Letters and Sounds.

Each book has been created to provide the best possible reading and learning experience. Our aim is to share our love of books with children, providing both emerging readers and prolific page-turners with beautiful books that are guaranteed to provoke interest and learning, regardless of ability.

BOOK BAND GRADED using the Institute of Education's approach to levelling.

PHONETICALLY DECODABLE supporting each phase of Letters and Sounds.

EXERCISES AND QUESTIONS to offer reinforcement and to ascertain comprehension.

BEAUTIFULLY ILLUSTRATED to inspire and provoke engagement, providing a variety of styles for the reader to enjoy whilst reading through the series.

AUTHOR INSIGHT:
EMILIE DUFRESNE

Born in Québec, Canada, Emilie Dufresne's academic achievements explain the knowledge and creativity that can be found in her books. At a young age, she received the award of Norfolk County Scholar, recognising her top grades in school. At the University of Kent, Emilie obtained a First Class Honours degree in English and American Literature, and was awarded a Masters in The Contemporary with Distinction. She has published over 60 books with BookLife Publishing, ranging from science to geography, art and sports, and even animals as superheroes! Children enjoy Emilie's books because of the detailed narrative and the engaging way she writes, which always makes children want to learn more.

This book focuses on the phonemes /o_e/ and /u_e/ and is an orange level 6 book band.